Unspoken Feelings
Of a Gentleman

Inspired by:

You

Written by:

Me

Cover design: Omar Rodriguez (Astute Productions)

Editors: Orlando Barajas, Kate Drilling, Katherine Vance

Photography: Omar Rodriguez (Astute Productions)

Artwork: TreManda Pewett

For more information, please visit

Gentlemenhood.com or

contact@gentlemenhood.com

ISBN-13: 978-0-9862556-0-1

Other books
By Pierre Alex Jeanty:

To The Women I Once Loved
ISBN - 978-0-9862556-3-2

Unspoken Feelings of a Gentleman II
ISBN-13: 978-0-9862556-7-0

Dedication

To GOD,

The real MVP

To my mother,

The number one example of a strong woman to me

The woman who contributed so much to my growth

To my sisters,

The women who raised me, women who have always loved and protected me

To my nieces,

Learn from the man who I was, and the man I am becoming. Learn about men from my story.

To my nephews,

Let my life be an example to you as well. Learn from my mistakes.

To my exes,

I thank you all for the experiences and lessons.

To my friends,

Carl Elie, Rene Saint-Preux, Kirsten Dimicco, Homer Betancourt, Iztchel Segoviano, Ana Martinez and many more, Thank you for believing in me.

To you, THE READERS,

The support you offer to me is second to none. You are the reason. Knowing you would be reading this text, I decided to overcome the feeling of not being a good enough writer, the fear of sharing intimate parts of my life, and the fear of exposing my vulnerability. I spent sleepless nights creating something to which I hope you can relate, learn and draw inspiration. YOU are my inspiration.

I deserve the right to be human.

Contents

Reader Disclaimer:

What you get out of this book is *your* choice.

Warning: This book may challenge you.

Introduction

These are the thoughts of a gentleman. Not a perfect man, but a gentleman. These are thoughts of a man who never saw the freedom in "freedom of speech" until now. These are the thoughts behind the anger, silence, pain, joy, smiles, sadness, betrayal and everything this journey called life can present. These are the thoughts of a man who can relate to most men.

No different than any other man, my journey consists of bottled up emotions and raw feelings that I've kept caged. I felt expressing my feelings would only exhibit weakness. I always felt misunderstood. I felt as if communicating my feelings would only be misconstrued by my listeners. I hated expressing myself, explaining myself, repeating myself. I hated communicating the deep parts of me. To compensate, I imprisoned all emotions inside, to be kept raw and unseen. How naïve of me!? I failed to see the destruction it placed in my path, the confusion it created between my loved ones and me.

Suppressing my emotions and true feelings led me to live many years with pain having complete control over me. Anger ordered my steps, and pride turned me cold - unwilling and unable to love. I spent most of my days as a troubled young man searching for happiness in all the wrong places. My heart was clogged with so many false beliefs of what a man should be according to society's standards. I believed that there was no room for any good to reside in it.

As a result, most of my relationships were unhealthy. I am a living testimony of the old adage, "Hurt people hurt people." I transferred the hurt that consumed me to a fair amount of women. I built walls after walls that kept going higher and higher, and with each experience worsened. Numerous relationship issues went unresolved because of the way I operated. I never wanted to express myself and be the real me. I refused to open up to anyone. Resentment filled my heart, which grew colder, which started to make me numb to love. After years of failing to find love, seeking it in all the wrong places, with a soul overflowing with unexpressed emotions and pain, I finally broke down. After losing a woman to whom I was engaged, and another whom I believed was my soul mate, I began to reevaluate. A pattern was present: women broke up with me because they were dating a lifeless soul who always got defensive, was unaffectionate, quick to anger, competitive and arrogant. I was toxic inside and it was burning everything good that came my way. This started a spiritual journey that led me to look into the mirror, look deep inside myself, identify my problems, and work towards fixing them.

Now, my silence has a voice. Expressing myself has become an escape for me, a necessity. Vulnerability is something of which I am no longer afraid. I have decided to start being real with myself and the people in my life. This book is dedicated to the men who feel helpless and think they have no one to whom they can express themselves. This is for the fellas who feel misunderstood, who are misguided by society. To the men trying to right their wrongs and open themselves to healthier relationships in the future. This book is also for the women who wonder what's inside the heads of men like me. It's for the women who've been hurt by men like me, and those who are in love with men who were once no different than I.

*Being a male
is inevitable,
a matter of birth.*

*Being a man
is a choice,
a matter of decisions.*

*Being a gentleman
is a matter of
perspective.*

Why

Men don't feel the need to express their feelings because they are taught that feelings are a weakness. A society full of prideful individuals contributes to this false idea of manhood that is downloaded into boys at a young age. We are allowed to voice fun (talk about cars, girls, clothes, money etc.), hate, violence, success . . . voice everything that reflects our strengths and foolishness. Weakness, however, should never be shown nor mentioned, unless in an attempt to point it out in another man. Weakness to me, was a foreign thing that can be found in women. We are taught the wrong things about weakness and what it truly means to be weak. We subconsciously pick up the idea that exposing our weaknesses makes us vulnerable, and vulnerability to anyone is the ultimate weakness. We have to be robots, heartless like Ironman. Society has infiltrated our minds with the wrong ideas of what a man is, and fed our brains inaccurate and inappropriate perceptions of manhood.

Weakness is actually the *fear* of looking weak, of not being perfect and strong. We invest our time and energy into not looking "soft", emotional or feminine, because we are afraid. We spend our childhoods giving in to false ideas of masculinity that built up false confidence, (especially when it comes to girls.) Instead of praising the girl who deep down makes us feel loved, touches our souls, and challenges our minds, we brag about the girls we manipulate into sleeping with us. This is what we were taught to believe was "manly." Speaking about the raw emotions in our lives is insignificant unless we're talking about sex. Our fear of appearing weak has blinded us to all fears that live within us. Even when we say we have no fear, we are fear driven. We boldly say, "Fear no man," meanwhile, fear spills out of us because we fear the man in the mirror who has flaws and weaknesses. He feels pain, is imperfect, and is the enemy of the man society wants us to be.

We were never taught that acknowledging our weaknesses opens the doors for strength. Sharing our weaknesses with loved ones opens the door for guidance and help. Being sensitive, emotional, catering to a woman we love, and embracing feminine attributes can be positive and strong forces in our lives, *if* we allow it. There is nothing wrong with showing "weakness".

Being insensitive is more of a sign of weakness than being sensitive.

Women try to understand men and men try to figure out women. Both sexes see each other as "Mission: Impossible" and a difficult maze. Many problems could be easily quelled if they would just be raw and open with each other.

One of the reasons relationships fail is because we are afraid to express our true feelings to our loved ones. A lack of communication can be a major issue in both platonic and romantic relationships. In most of my relationships, I spent most of the time trying to figure out the hints my girlfriends would give and they would try to figure out what was on my mind when my lips were closed. Existing this way, everything became a game. The goal became getting one another to express how we truly feel. Communication is one of the most important ingredients in any relationship, but in my mouth it left a bitter taste. Mind games and closed lips have ruined nearly all my relationships; I was a man of few words, yet, many issues.

A major contributor to the lack of communication between men and women is technology, which has hindered our ability to relay true emotions. Prior to technology there was a communication barrier but never was it to this level. Because of technology, real interaction doesn't take place as often as it should. We hide behind texts, emails, Facebook, Twitter, etc. We find it hard to communicate real feelings, engage in heartfelt conversations, or connect intimately. Sadly, most of us don't see the lack of effectiveness through these modern ways of communication. As a result, most relationships hardly mature past the beginning "fling" stage. They never reach the point where partners truly learn each other and have a deep connection. Everything simply stays on the surface. Relationships are being destroyed by impersonal conversations, misinterpreted tones and text messages, "I love you," (with no real feelings behind the phrase), and so forth.

I've learned the hard way how cancerous a lack of communication can be. I locked away feelings deep within my soul and didn't express emotions, which produced nothing but pain and bad results in my life. This is also happening in several other lives. Many girlfriends would die to have their man spill his heart out just once. Countless wives are hoping their spouse would just call from time to time and say, "I love you," instead of texting on the go. Numerous men are tired of bottling up their emotions, but don't know how or where to express them. People just want to be heard, want to feel understood, and want to share their hearts without feeling that their vulnerability is ammo for the "enemy."

I love you

We've been through so much together

I've seen you grow into someone you thought you'd never be

I've seen you endure challenges most will never see

Mocked by your peers for being from a different culture

Feeling deserted, you searched for ways to adapt and become accepted

You resorted to fitting in instead of making a stand for your true self

You've made countless mistakes in pursuit of acceptance

To me, it was undeniable you were meant to be a misfit

You dove into finding your talents and utilizing them

Unapologetically, you began making your mark during your middle school years

Discovering your skills as a runner made a way for you to flee from the norm

Racing hard and your pace in this life

Hurdle after hurdle, you never stopped jumping and running towards the finish line

You lost focus numerous times running someone else's race, matching their suicidal pace, but over time you opened your eyes and ran your race in your lane

You used failures as your stepping stone to climb up to where you are now and where you're going

I love you, I love you even when you hate you

Thank you for staying true to you, never justifying your flaws and running away from your consequences

You've taught me so much.

 I'm proud of you

I love you so much.

Thank you for being a friend, an example, a brother

 Thank you for being the man you are now.

I love you, man in the mirror

The day you begin to accept who you are is when the journey of knowing yourself begins. That day is when validation through others becomes something of the past, and loving you and evolving into who you were made to be will begin.

Dear Dad

I forgive you.

I forgive you for giving your seed to my mother and disappearing.

I forgive you for not understanding that every seed you plant needs to be taken care of. I needed to be watered by your love, exposed to the light of manhood from you, fertilized by your discipline and grown into your image.

I forgive you for not being a co-parent with my mother. She played Superwoman and Superman while you were busy trying to find your identity as Clark Kent.

I forgive you for not being here to teach me about girls, sports...life. You were supposed to be here for me to learn from your mistakes.

I forgive you for teaching me my first lessons about being a boy. Having your way with my mother and abandoning her taught me irresponsibility and immaturity.

I forgive you for being a ghost throughout my entire life journey--visiting sometimes to confirm you existed, but not long enough for me to believe.

I forgive you for your mistakes. While you were incarcerated, I was chained by the feelings of unworthiness and imprisoned by my insecurities. The pain of your absence trapped me in the prison cell of my own skin.

After being impregnated by resentments for more than nine months, the forgiveness in me for you was born.

I forgive you.

Wherever your soul resides now, be it Heaven or hell, know that your son has forgiven you.

Sincerely,

Your healed son

It takes a man to raise a man. The lack of a father's presence is destroying some boys, and has caused many men to take the poor routes they've taken – full of violence and bad choices. Absent fathers rob children of love, affection, and support from a man.

Most men fear expressing their love for another man, believing the act is too feminine-- except when a loved one is dying. They believe in showing tough love, but never showing any real love. Some men are convinced love should only be displayed when the recipient is on the verge of giving up all hope that love exists at all. When a little boy tearfully asks if his father loves him, the man will begrudgingly show some affection, but only enough to make the tears stop. Men fear that affection toward another man will be perceived as a homosexual advance. Even now, it's hard for me to utter the words "I love you" to another man. It doesn't matter whether it's a friend I love dearly or a male family member for whom I would die. This is because I was denied the experience and example of a father's love. Many young men have never seen a display of unconditional and unadulterated love between men (and/or women!), so they're ignorant about its significance and essential nature, tending only to express the opposite. Not only do these young men have anger and hate in their hearts toward their fathers, they have no one close to them to whom they can express their feelings. I personally believed that my mother wouldn't understand if I told her how I felt, friends wouldn't listen to me unless the topic was about sports, music, banging women or anything unrelated to love. Like many males, I got accustomed to showing no love, became numb to the pain, and learned to live with it.

 In search of love, affection, support and identity, I looked for those things in women. I used sex as a facade of love for them. I picked the prettiest and the most successful girls I could win over, and let them define me. I wanted to be "the man", because "the man" was loved and the women I had around me perfected that image. It was an image created from the lack of a positive masculine figure in my life. I continually searched for it in all the wrong places, eventually making pop-culture figures my go-to solution. I let rappers shape the image of a man in my head with the way they portrayed manhood in their songs. I believed a male wasn't a man unless he had an untouchable demeanor, cars, women, and clothes – something I remember hearing in one of Drake's songs during my college days. These men became my idols despite their having no direction, love, happiness, or true success. They were just like me and of all ages. They were an image of what I would become if I continued down my current path.

I was able to change my path in the midst of the storm of teenage confusion. Following my father's death, when I met regularly with my high school counselor, he took me under his wing and taught me the importance of education, humility, and being an optimist. He made me value life more and drove me to do more for myself than I had any intention of doing. I later met an older gentleman who became my mentor; he taught me manners and gave me an example of true success. He and his wife grew up not having much, but ended up developing a successful food delivery company and retired early. Since then, he's devoted himself to mentoring high school kids who have a hunger to rise above mediocrity. I guess that group of kids of which I was a part, reminded him of his younger self. Then, I met my church's associate pastor, who exemplified a man of God who isn't perfect, but strives daily to live a holy life. He taught me accountability, how to have a real relationship with Jesus Christ by committing to the Lord's ways, and how to be a good husband.

These men instilled the core values I was missing because of my father's absence. Although a mother can do a great job playing both roles, there's a lot a man can learn only from another man. Ideally, that man should be his father – it is vital for men to take care of their seeds. Being able to find other father figures is essential for fatherless boys to develop into men.

Too many baby daddies not enough fathers

Too many rappers not enough role models

Too many entertainers not enough educators

Too many preachers not enough spirit-led men

To The Queen

I love you

When I hear you talk about the obstacles you faced to have me, I sit in awe

Although my face looks expressionless, inside I feel every word

When I hear you explain what it took to provide for me, all I can say is "I can never repay you"

After I was born you had to abandon me when I was months old

Only to travel to the U.S to keep chasing the American dream and provide for us

You sacrificed so much with the little you had

The four years you were gone did have me question your love for me

I had no father around and a mother who would visit like most fathers do nowadays

I felt disowned

My sisters constantly reminded me how much you were sacrificing to provide for us

Void of understanding in my younger days, it didn't matter

I wanted you in my childhood

Fast forward to now, that's why I seem so distant most times

I feel like I don't know you although you're my mother

All I knew then is what I know now with better understanding

I know you are business minded, loving and that you cherish me, your only son

But that's it

I'm just thankful you took on the job of my father without a complaint

You are a fighter and a survivor

And overcoming breast cancer was more than proof to me

I am grateful that throughout your cancer process you saw my heart

You saw past the unaffectionate and stubborn side of me

I am glad that the sacrifice I've made for you is evidence enough that I do love you

Sadly, it took that for me to express how important you are to me

It's just that I never knew how to love. You and Dad were never around to show me love

My sister's care for me was the closest thing to love I've known

But despite it all, I love you

Through maturity I've learned to love, appreciate and value you

It burns me inside that I am not able to help you retire

That's why when you ask for my help, I react wrong sometimes because I want you to be living right

Living how a mother should be living once her children are grown

Work free, stress free and bill free

That time has yet to arrive, but I promise you, it'll come

I love you

The exact replica of you I am, the boy version

We argue sometimes because we are too alike

Fight for a minute and the next we are completely all right

If there's anything I want you to know before you leave to be in the presence of the Almighty,

I love you way more than it shows

Thank you for being such a warrior and great provider

Your strength is equal to that of one thousand men

Again, I thank you, my Queen

Who you become in life isn't determined by the circumstances you face, it is determined by the decisions you make in response to your circumstances.

I refuse to let my mistakes define me. When they (the people who do not believe in me) see me, they see how many times I've fallen as a man. All they see is a failure. When I see how many times I've fallen, I see chances to succeed. I've been a fool who made plenty of bad decisions. I've been an idiot, stuck in my own ways. I've been a prideful individual, living as a know-it-all. The more I live, the more I make changes for the better. The more I live, the more I open myself to corrections, the more I evolve, the more I become who God says I am to be in the Bible. Every day, I look in the mirror, and I see someone who has failed countless times, but I also see a fella striving to be a gentleman; a fella who refuses to stay down. I may not have been a solid guy my entire life, but the concrete truth is that I will never let my failures defeat me. Mock me, say I will never change, throw dirt on my name.... I will rise above every bad choice, every foolish decision, and every bad experience. I will continue to grow into the good man I ought to be.

To the doubters and the mockers,

She Was My First

She was my first crush past the innocent stage

The first girl who made my heart beat at the pace of Usain Bolt

Beat after beat, she made my heart skip

I wrote a letter to let her know how I admired everything about her being

It wasn't a gentlemanly gesture, but a 6th grader's way of expressing his feelings to his crush

Once she discovered my desire for her, she opened to letting me discover her

We walked to class together, got on the bus together and sat with each other

A love grew inside me

I carried an extra shirt at all times just in case it happened to be cold

As my shirts wrapped around her body to supply her with necessary heat on the cold days, she felt rescued and secure

I envisioned my arms being wrapped around her the same way

I graduated to using my lunch money to buy her snacks at lunch time

Consistently arrived at school at an early time to make myself available for her

What a perfect way to start my day: with the one who made my heart smile and brighten up my day

I craved her attention and would do anything for her to fall for me

Besides, everyone I knew belonged to someone, so, I wanted someone too

Until one winter day, my heart started to grow cold, and the idea of belonging to someone became one for fools

A friend of mine noticed the attention I gave her

He traced my routines and told me I labored too much to win over this girl: ("I'll show you how to get this girl in no time")

I wasn't a skilled player

My mind couldn't bring to life clever words to convince her with well-decorated lies

He was a master at spitting game.

He was skilled at manipulation after being tutored by his older brothers who made him this smooth operator

He approached her in my absence

Endorsed by popularity, and empowered by his words that were smoother than oil, he scored in a matter of minutes, while with me, her guard was up so high, it seemed like I never had a shot

I vanished out of her mind in a matter of hours

All my efforts, nice gestures, loving ways were too insufficient for me to win her heart

Confusion consumed me

The first girl my heart chose, chose someone else

Someone who didn't even have his heart in it.

Our experiences shape who we are. Behind every bad guy is a trail of experiences that made him believe being bad would benefit him more than would being a good person. Starting at a young age, I was taught to be a "good guy," but later, I started distancing myself from that. Being very well disciplined by sisters, and taught to value women by my mother, it would have been unheard of for me to approach women with anything but respect. It was hard for me to approach *anyone* impolitely. I was raised with manners. I was raised to be a gentleman. The only problem was that the culture I was raised *for* wasn't the culture I was being raised *in*. I was a Haitian kid growing up in America and there was a disconnect.

I was too nice, too gentle. I was too considerate and too forgiving. I wasn't popular or smooth. I only knew to be honest and polite. Sadly, that was also a deterrent to attaining a girlfriend of my choosing. It wasn't what girls I encountered were used to or what they wanted. From what I could perceive, they wanted a man to make them feel pretty with lies, and loved without evidence. They wanted the alpha male who every woman wanted and every man wanted to emulate. However, I offered something different. I was a different type. I was the type to ask the girls to dance instead of jumping behind them and inappropriately touching them. I wasn't even used to girls shaking their butts on me, to be honest. I was the type to buy girls gifts, ask for dates, "act right" and treat them well. I was the type to fall in love before I did anything. But this was the wrong type for the girls I was eyeing. I was the "wrong type" as a teenager, and I am still today. Females do still appreciate the type of man I am, but never picture themselves with me. Those are the type of women I've chased-- trying to make sense of why they appreciated who I am, but couldn't fall for me.

After receiving many rejections and being taken advantage of for being "the nice guy," by the women with whom I was able to "get lucky," my heart hardened.

As I grew up, (physically, not mentally), I began living and behaving like a jerk. I became an elite athlete and a cut-throat fella. I was still respectful toward my peers, but sarcastic and mean to girls; especially the ones who had my interest. This behavior was received and loved by the people around me. When it came to immature girls with attitudes, they were most responsive to my alpha male treatment and attitude. I knew how to shut them up, and treated them as if they were disposable. They wanted to work to prove themselves to me and be accepted. They loved me talking dirty to them and being a jerk in texts and when I would deny them in public. They loved the false promises, attention, and cockiness and so on. I couldn't help myself, and being the bad guy was a simple choice because it was the only thing that worked for me. It was the only thing that made me feel appreciated for who I was, even though that person wasn't truly me.

Most of my life, I neglected the good guy who I knew I was. I stuck with the bad guy routine, because it was the only role with seeming credibility; the only persona that made me successful at getting the women who I wanted. The bad guy was the only one everyone applauded. The bad guy was apparently the only one who was worthy of everyone's attention. The experiences I've had (starting with the first girl I cared for choosing a "player," over me,) made me *that* guy. For a long time, I lived as this guy. It was easy being that guy.

As I matured into the man who I am now, I began to recognize my poor decisions. The women I chased weren't women, but girls, who wanted the bad guys in their lives. I overlooked quality women because I was chasing the wrong females for the wrong reasons. My idea of a quality woman was as off-base as that of the bad boy-chasing girls' idea of a solid male. It was the negative consequences of my poor decisions that led me down the wrong path.

Don't stop doing the nice things that the wrong women failed to appreciate. They'll mean the world to the right woman.

Feelings of a Pimp

They think I was a player because I was devoted to the
game
They thought I worked hard on my offense to break down
these women's defenses just to score
They think it's the body count that made me manipulate
them into my arms to get between their legs
They think I'm satisfied with a different woman in my bed
every night

When during the day, even my bed can feel the loneliness
They think I love the easy women
They think it's for the cool points that my heart grew cold
They think they have me figured out

Another dog chasing after every female dog in the streets
They think I'm happy with all the texting buddies, but no
wife

But they don't know
They don't know how tired I am of this, how tired I am of
myself
How tired I am of living like this
How tired I am of these games, but that's the only way I
can score with a chick
They don't know how after sleeping with these ladies, I
wish I had more chemistry with at least one of them to
cuddle, to give goodnight kisses and wake up beside

They don't know how loneliness consumes me
With a phone filled with women's numbers, I still feel
unwanted and unworthy

They don't know these easy women make it easy for me to
feel confident about myself; although it's the wrong type
of confidence

I feel validated by them, I feel accomplished, I feel loved
although I'm having sex with them, not making love
They don't know how tired I am of chasing fool's gold

Chasing fast women who would sleep with me in a
heartbeat
Leaving me with the empty feeling I felt before I started
the chase
The player in me is played out. I just want love, but that's
the only thing I can't seem to find
So, I keep pimping in hope of finding love

Her insecurities were beautiful
They opened the door for me as an opportunist
She was the perfect candidate
Oh so sweet, but oh so hurt
How smart would I be if I didn't capitalize?
Some fellas get women drunk and have their way with them
I was doing nothing wrong but pretending to be prince charming, just to get the same results

I became what they needed emotionally
 I was the shoulder to cry on, the ear to listen to, the one person who understood
I was a smooth criminal manipulating the innocent

Did not feel an ounce of guilt because I was weak myself
I was insecure
 I couldn't help preying on vulnerable women
In their weakness I found strength
I was a coward, a "wannabe" player
I was playing the wrong games, winning the wrong prizes

The truth is, no strong man takes advantage of a woman's vulnerability. It is a trait of the weak.

Diary of a Weak Man

Our cries for acceptance create the rivers in which we drown our identities.

Cool

Cool. That is the word that contributed to my cold heart. Nothing validated who I was more than the "cool points" I acquired as a young man, or so I thought. The numbers had to be earned. I had to get the phone numbers of and sleep with enough women. Rejection from women who didn't find me good enough had to burn.

I gave my heart and soul to athletics as a young man because it made me *cool*. I was ashamed of the fact that I waited until I was considered an adult to start having sex. Being an 18 year old who hadn't had sex wasn't *cool*. Knowing this, I spent countless hours on Myspace™ during my high school years sending the same well-prepared message to every girl in my vicinity, hoping a few would surrender their numbers (and possibly more) to me. The more fish I caught, the more *cool* it made me. I texted girls nudes, fishing for compliments to boost my self-esteem and make me feel *cool*. I traveled long ways in search of sex to meet up with older females who believed in the talk I talked. Catching a cougar is what I believed made me *cool*.

I risked everything for "cool." I did anything that would earn me cool points. I wanted to be known as a successful "mac daddy" to the guys, and Mr. Casanova to the gals. I devoted myself to building up my stats with women to share stories with others, so they would know that I was *the man*. I wanted to be the cool dude and saw nothing wrong with manipulating and using women. I had an agenda, and I thought I wasn't wrong because they succumbed by choice.

As men, many of us do what we believe makes us stand out as the ultimate alpha male.

Men (and even women) want to be noticed. We may not verbalize our thirst for attention, but our actions often indicate that craving. Some do the wrong thing to attract attention, and some just do the wrong thing. The fact is, we all crave attention and many of us will do anything to get it. *"Our cries for acceptance create the rivers in which we drown our identities."*

We spend too much time trying to fit in. From a young age, we try doing things we see everyone else doing – what we believe to be cool and acceptable. As we grow into adults, some of us still do what we see others doing, but claim it's far different. These days, we have too many individuals putting far too much effort into standing out. Many guys claim their swag is "so impeccable, no one can touch it," despite all of their cohorts owning the same pairs of Jordan shoes, and the same expensive belts they claim no one else owns. "Standing out" doesn't always mean aesthetically. To stand out, you have to live your life *your* way. You have to be mature, and you have to be the man God created you to be. We are all different and if we all live *our* lives, instead of imitating the lives of others, we can all contribute something different to this world.

"Cool" is what keeps many from letting go the desires of their egos, even when they know it is destructive. Without the idea of "cool," some men would mature faster and settle down sooner, but in their thirst for relevance, they have to be…cool. When a man gets married or enters a committed relationship, some of his peers often say things like "I don't know how you sleep with the same woman," or, "I couldn't do it." …"Your girl got you whipped…" just because that man can't hang out whenever his friends want him to hang out. Men hear the comments of their single immature friends and start to question themselves and their decisions. Settling down can be great to them and they love it. On the contrary, the feeling of missing out, of being excluded from fun, not being cool anymore…causes many to venture off into foolish ventures that destroy their relationships. Honoring the same woman may be the right thing to do in their mind, but it doesn't fit the idea of cool, so it's not fun.

Until a man grows out of the idea that he has to be cool, he will never win with those who he thinks are cool.

He shouldn't try to be cool, he should try to be himself.

*There comes a time when a man will graduate from thinking, **"love is for suckas"** to becoming himself, **"a sucka for love."***

Boredom

The person who brings life to my evil desires
The state where most of my thoughtless decisions started
The reason I started conversations with so many women
who I ended up using
The reason behind all the nights I spent decreasing my
sperm count
The force behind the drives to become intoxicated
The friend who introduced me to "Madame Mary Jane"
The main influencer that caused me to get on my Apple
phone, do some private browsing, and watch these Eves
undress themselves and sex away
Because of you, my thoughts will wander and take
command from the devil
Because of you, I've made choices that made me seem so
evil
When the consequences start to pile up,
I ask myself "why?" And then I remember, I was bored.

Influence

"He who lies with dogs rises with fleas."

Surround yourself with immature males who see women as pieces of meat, and you'll act like a dog.

You never touched a girl there before? You never had this done to you? What about this position or that position?

Questions like these always had me doubting myself as a teen. My peers made me question myself as a young man. I felt as though I was not complete for lacking sexual experience. I felt like I was a failure for waiting until I was eighteen years old to lose my virginity. I ended up having sex because of peer pressure. I lost my virginity because it was an act that I thought would make me like every person in my circle. Peer pressure is the reason I've done many things in my life. It doesn't come by force, it comes by influence. Because of peer pressure, I stopped believing in waiting until marriage. I gave in to alcohol, marijuana, and a few other activities that aren't part of who I wanted (or want) to be, but I caved into them anyway because of guilt. By guilt, I mean, feeling as if I was doing something wrong for not believing the same as the people around me and acting accordingly. I was a rebel at heart and always desired to be different, so eventually giving in to the things other people did was an easy option.

Out of my circle of four close friends in high school, the one with whom I was closest, was also good friends with some acquaintances outside our circle. They introduced him to the fast lifestyle, and made him feel that he should be living the same way, He started having sex consistently; running games on women. Once he started, it was in no time that the rest of us followed.

The power of influence is greater than many of us believe. Who I spent my time with helped shape me into who I became. The people anyone chooses to keep in his or her circle will become influences.

The company I kept when I was a young man was very different to those with whom I spend time now. I can't contend to be a great husband in the future, practice celibacy, and be devoted to my spiritual life, if I consistently keep myself in the presence of friends who are promiscuous, live in the clubs and have carefree lifestyles. Eventually, I would likely fall into their lifestyle, because what they are doing is more enticing It is what our flesh desire because it's fun, doesn't promote morality, discipline and maturity. I will be far more tempted and willing to do the things they practice because it also fall under the umbrella of cool. The majority are partying, drinking, sexing, drugging and it seems fun, it piques our interest, it makes us living opposite feel left out and curious at times but it's also lead to the path of destruction, leads down a sorrow path of brokenness and unhappiness. It is why we must watch who is in our circle. The Bible says, "Bad Company corrupts good character" and for me it is necessary to keep a group of well-rounded individuals around me to make me better.

I cried

My heart was overflowing

I could not contain it

I hated the feeling of breaking down, but it was my only option

I couldn't hold it anymore

I had enough

The world vacuumed the happiness out of my heart

I've harbored everything inside of me

It took me reaching the point where enough became enough

I cried, I wept like a baby

It was my last resort, the only thing I could do

After the tears flooded out of my eyes, all I could do was release the sounds of anger, disappointment, defeat and hate

But, I felt free

It was as if life re-entered my soul, the weight of the world fell off my back.

Peace began to swallow me

Uncertain about the outcome but there was a relief

I began to ask, "Why?" Why was I taught that this was only for "little girls" since I was a boy?

Why was it pounded in my head that boys don't cry when I felt the urge like everyone else?

Why was I told in every situation to man up and not cry? I'd manned up all my life and now my strength to stay tough broke down

I felt robbed of a remedy to my pain

I felt lied to about what it meant for a man to cry

They told me to hold in these tears that would've flushed out my clogged heart, instead of spilling all this poison into other's lives as my escape

Only if I knew, I wouldn't let all these emotions build up until I broke down

It wasn't a crime to cry

It was a crime that they've made me hold in these tears and filter it out in all the negative ways

Projecting my anger on anyone I could make a victim

Only if they knew how much of an injustice that was to me and the people I took my hurt out on

Crying did not solve my issues nor did it mend my brokenness, but it lightened the load on my soul

Men ought to cry because men are real people, with real feelings, real emotions

Men deal with pressures in life: broken hearts and persecution

I did not fight the moments where I couldn't do anything but cry

I embraced it and cried my heart out

I cried

Half Naked

When her girls saw her in that dress, they saw cuteness

When my boys and I saw her, we saw an invitation to feast

The way she presented herself made her appear as a piece of meat in our eyes, and we turned into dogs drooling over a bone

We were hunters and we would chase and prey on the weak

...an easy meal was all we saw

King of the jungle felt like a lion that had a zebra cornered

Whether she was aware or not, the fact is: the less skin she covered, the more she would be preyed on by immature boys like me

I watched her with lusting eyes

The more skin she showed, the less I imagined, the more I assumed she was fishing for attention

I wanted to do some things to her

From the porn stars to the stripper, I couldn't tell them apart from her

The tighter the dress the tighter my game

The more creative I became with my words and the more ready I became to attack her mind.

The way she dressed screamed vulnerability and that was what I wanted

As I looked at her and envisioned her in my bed

She looked as if she was already prepared, and undressing her would be half of the job

A couple of foul words might bring the freak out of her

Sexually, that's the only way I believed I should approach her

"Why should I even respect her if she doesn't respect herself?"

"Why should I approach her like a queen if she is presenting herself as a harlot?"

Smooth operator, my game plan was guaranteed a win

Only to face rejection

I felt cheated because her appearance contradicted what I expected

"Why would she dress like that if she wanted to be respected?"

Dressing in a way that is sexually suggestive attracts immature males. Many girls hate that, but it is a sad reality. We all wish we could live in a world where everyone looked past our outer appearances and focused on our inner being. The only likely way for that to happen is if someone is on a journey of loving us. A first impression does make a lasting impression; sometimes it defines us to a person we'll never see again.

The way a woman dressed determined the way I treated her

Unfortunately, a lot of males are hunters and will prey on girls. Like a lion who's starving, men who operated the way I used to operate used the process of elimination when it came to finding someone to sleep with...narrowing down the herd to it's weakest link. During my younger days, I judged girls and mastered the art of finding the one to hook up with at the parties and take home later on. I was by no means a lady's, man, but I knew enough to score at the end of most party nights during my college years. At every party, it was evident which ones to target – the ones with the fewest clothes who seemed to have had the most alcohol. It's unfortunate that I used to be that way, but as a young man looking for fun, I chose to target what was easy, and in most cases, the women who appeared easy were exactly that.

As I matured, I stopped chasing women who dressed up for one-night stands, and started to pursue older women who seemed to be out of that stage. These women dressed in a way that wouldn't invite slobbering, immature men into bed. They didn't care for attention. They knew what they wanted and were not settling for less. They presented themselves with class. Many of them were old fashioned, raised in the days where women were supposed to appear more conservative. These women challenged my mind and most led me to treat them with respect due to the amount of self-respect they had. Their standards being higher helped elevate me to become a better man. The way they carried themselves was attractive to me. They had my attention. I opened up to the idea of pursuing them. I worked to win them over. I put in the effort. I valued my relationships more with them than with anyone else. They influenced me and contributed into my maturity. From my experiences with them, I learned the value of a good woman in a man's life.

When I didn't have any self-respect, I disrespected women who I felt were disrespecting themselves. When I wasn't looking for anything serious, I gave those women the attention they seemed to crave because they would most likely give me what I wanted. As I grew to love and respect myself more, I also grew to be more caring and loving towards others- especially women. Instead of being a dog toward them, I felt compelled to treat them with respect. As I evolved more into the man I was made to be, I began to treat people more like I wanted to be treated. I wanted to be respected, not judged. Supported, not sheltered. This is how I continuously strive to treat others – women or men.

Part of me

The part of me that loves you is the part of me I've been conditioned to deny

The delicate part that drives me to soften up to every touch

The part of me that wanted my walls to come down

This part of me they told me to never expose

This part of me was welcoming to love

This part of me was empathetic

This part of me was one you could explore

This part of me is the part only the right woman would seek and find

This part of me was vulnerable, willing to love no matter what

It was opened to happiness, joy, peace

This part of me was willing to sacrifice anything without fear

This part of me was the part you needed me to share with you

This part of me was the part I hid from you.

My Ego Cheated

I felt all of me falling in love with you

But my ego reminded me of all the things I've been through

Mocked for being different

Hurt for being nice

Rejected because I genuinely cared

The only one who befriended me, cared for me, accepted me and loved me was my ego

He told me being a jerk was the way to win

I believed him because I saw it in action all around me

He told me to forget love, and just sex them

I became sold on sex because sex sells and it seemed that's what these girls were buying

He reminded me how much rejection I faced for being the nice guy

I grew colder than winter

The bad boy in me started growing up

I started exploring the darkest parts, of me and listening to the dog in me

A womanizer I became

It built in me the wrong sense of pride

In love, I lost hope

The idea of love that this society embedded
was what I started believing in

It was all about saying "I love you" and sexing _____ ...had
you whispering those words back to me

Falling in lust rather than love

I indulged in pop culture

I treated women how these boys treated them on the
regular

When you entered the picture you were already tainted in
my mind

I was used to showing just enough interest where I felt I
couldn't be played

I was used to showing I cared but not enough to care if
they left

I was used to showing people that I can love them, but if
they hurt me, I can hurt them back

My ego was my best friend, my brother, my teacher

It had me harden my heart toward love and

Glorified the wrong in me

It made me quick to protect myself; defensive, so when I
felt myself loving you, he spoke up

He pointed out everything you did wrong

He gossiped with me about you

He bashed you

He encouraged me to entertain women because it wasn't guaranteed you wouldn't hurt me

When you started nagging about what I wasn't doing right, my ego built a case to prove you weren't worth committing to

Your cry for attention and affection from me turned burdensome with his input

When you finally got another man involved

He, (*my ego*) whispered to my doubts and fears, he made me feel as if pain was what I was going to settle for

He awakened my anger, gave life to the selfishness and resurrected the foolishness in me that started to die with you

He gave me enough evidence to find you guilty and punish you by being worse

I listened to him and cheated

Wasn't the temptation, wasn't her look, wasn't a connection between us

It was my ego

He hated you, hated your love for me and hated what we could be

It was my ego

My ego cheated on you

I've been a cheater, but I've never been a cheater because I found better. I cheated because I was too egotistical to allow anyone to win my heart. I didn't want to be vulnerable or too open to hurt and heartbreak.

Cheating was always a way of my showing to my partners that I could go out and find someone new if they ever did anything wrong to me. It was a warning-- the most foolish warning I could give. What I learned from my generation is to never love too hard. To never show anyone you can't live without them. It's always about who can survive without the other while attempting to commit to each other. It's a very contradicting mindset.

In me existed this misguided idea of a power couple. To me a "power couple" was two people who look good enough to attract anyone, able to have sarcastic battles with each other without leaving emotional wounds, too independent for their own good, keeping their guards up. Compromising was a stupid thing to do. In my mind, power couples had to be independent, but not interdependent, which was a backward way of thinking. With this belief in relationships, it became a contest between us.

It was all about who could show they didn't need the other the most. Whatever they did to me provoked me to seek revenge and hurt them worse. It was always about being better and not looking weak. So when an ex mentioned to me how men hit on her, if the amount of women who hit on *me* didn't trump hers, I had to get my numbers up. I would fish for attention from women and flirted to get even. If she had a male friend she became too close to and didn't see what it was doing to the relationship, I would find a woman friend to confide in. If she kissed someone or "someone kissed her," as they say nowadays, I would find a woman willing to sleep with me anytime I wanted.

Many cheat because they fall into temptation and they don't care. While that was the case with me at times, it was mostly because I couldn't allow myself to come second in the relationship. I never wanted to work as a team. It was always a competition where everything had to be me, me, me, and never **WE**. When the opportunity arose to hurt and crush my partner to show her that no one should mess with me, I did it.

The woman of my dreams

Can't seem to get it right
Everything that I fight for tells me I'm fighting the
wrong fight
Seems like I'm always too late when it comes to winning
anyone back
Seems like this train is always heading down the wrong
track
Although giving up seems to be my best bet, I will keep
playing the wrong hand 'til I get my cards right
Eventually my queen will be in my hand,
and I'll be done playing the joker
I've learned by now in life you have to fail your way to
the top
I will continue to fail until I find my way to your heart

Deep regrets were heavy on my heart
My decisions are the reason you feel shattered
Keeping yourself together looking into my eyes while all
you feel inside is broken
Disappointed in yourself for believing in a man who
doesn't give a dang
Too cocky to be sentimental, and utter "sorry"
I can see the hurt occupy your eyes
I can feel the pain just looking at the state you're in
But I'm a man, I didn't need to say sorry
Foolish me
I watched you walk away without a word when everything
in me wanted to kneel down and cry out for forgiveness
You were the owner of my heart
The damages I did to you felt so much like self-destruction
So stubborn
I held my apology, my cry, my expression of deep regrets,
everything that would reassure you that my intentions
were never to hurt you
Foolish me
All I had to do was say I'm sorry and mean it
But I swallowed those words and watched you walk away.

I'm sorry

Infidelity

She was my most precious piece of land

My most valuable property

Her heart was the soil in which I planted my hope and love

Her mind was sunlight that provided the energy; that weeded out the fears, the doubts, and the negative energy.

Her soul was mine, together we were one

Her love was my most valuable asset

UNTIL a man invaded my property and walked over my land with a grin

Dang Grinch, stole my present

He watered her soil with manipulation, false hope and everything wrong but well-presented to a point she believed

Her mind was no longer providing the energy I needed

There was an eclipse in the way now

I was robbed, but my possession wasn't possessed

She freely gave herself to a man I never knew

I was cheated and felt bankrupt

The time, the energy, the hope, the love, the deep parts of me invested were all gone

My heart crashed, she left me to be one with him

When a woman cheats on a man, it is the ultimate disrespect to him. Women most likely feel disrespected as well if they're cheated on, but often to a man, it's the worst form of disrespect. It hits them hard and to the core. It's the highest level of disrespect because it's the lowest shot at his ego. When I dated a woman, she was mine and mine only. I was slow to invest my heart. I allowed myself to fall in love slower than the women I've been with because I wanted to make sure that this investment wasn't going to be taken away from me and hurt me later on. Women follow this protocol too, but generally, it usually takes a man far longer than a woman to invest his heart and allow himself to fall in love.

My idea of love was always respect but it seemed like the women I knew believed in a different definition.

Similar, I'm sure, but our versions weren't the same. Their idea of love was commitment, affection, monogamy; a love that gradually grows into being unconditional

Respect was part of their love because disrespect and love cannot co-exist, but respect wasn't the priority of their version of love. It wasn't the basis of their love stories which is why women tend to tolerate cheating more often than do than men.

My idea of love always involved respect, but it seemed as if the women I knew focused more on acceptance and grace rather than respect. For those women, love is kind, love is forgiving, love is long suffering, it sees well in every situation and so forth. The women I knew (and those represented in popular culture) are more likely to display these "honorable" characteristics of love when their partners aren't faithful and infidelity becomes commonplace. More women endure their partners' infidelity and are more open to forgiveness than are men. They stand by their men. It's rare for a man to take back his cheating ex and even more uncommon for him to stick around while being mistreated. I rarely saw a man endure anything in a relationship that disrespected his masculinity or ego. Anytime I fell in love, yes, emotions were involved and all the good that came with love was there. I surrendered my heart when I felt confident that those women respected me, and that they would not let any other man come take my throne at the top of their hearts. I had to feel secure.

When my girlfriend cheated on me, it took away my pride and my dignity; it was a direct attack to my ego and it insulted my manhood. It challenged my confidence. It was a loss in my never-ending checklist of wins and losses. We are competitive creatures, and some men are always trying to be better and do better than other men. Sometimes we subconsciously compete with each other. When a man came and took my woman, it was not only betrayal, but also defeat. The defeat stings the most. It's like working hard to build a house and someone comes and takes it from you without you being able to retaliate or resist. It'll hurt you, but the fact that you can't retaliate will make you feel weak, useless and worthless. It would be far better for you if they destroyed it, allowing you to rebuild, but taking it away when you can't do anything about it is different. You can heal from betrayal. Trust can be restored. Whatever is broken can be rebuilt if both put the effort in and are willing to start over from scratch. It's why a lot of men would rather bury the relationship and never attempt to revive it.

For some fellas, being with a woman can be somewhat about ownership. It was to me in the days when my ego ran my life. My girl was **my** girl and that was it. I made sure it stayed that way and no man can say they took my girl. You ought to protect your relationship and never settle for someone who cannot be loyal to you, but this way of thinking was possessive and objectified women.

This belief also contributes to males not respecting each other's relationships in the light of competition. The competitive nature of some guys motivates them to go after women who are already taken...makes those fellas feel more validated. It is one of those "If I'm able to take this girl from this guy, I'm the man" type of thing. It's a boost to one man's ego and an insult to another's. Your girl should securely be yours without another man being able to come in and take her. Hence the fact that "Mr. Steal your girl" is a popular title males want to inherit. Also in the hip hop world, which is a major influence on our generation, the ultimate disrespect to a man is another man sleeping with the woman who they claim to be theirs.

Women aren't objects. They aren't property men own but not all males see it that way. Many men are all about what's MINE - "my wife," "my girlfriend," "my chick," and other inappropriate titles that let people know that's their woman. We have put a value on women without actually valuing them. Some of us value them merely as possessions and some as an ultimate prize. That is why cheating is usually a direct attack to many men's manhood, it was to mine. Being cheated on was one of the things I dealt with that held me back for so long. I never wanted to let a woman put me in the position of feeling less than whole ever again. I kept my heart closed so I would never become a fool in anyone's eyes again; never be disrespected again. I was afraid of being a laughing stock after I was cheated on during my high school days by a girl who I kept around for benefits, but thought I had her on lock. (Looking back, I had no right to think of her as "mine", since I wasn't doing anything to make her want to stay around or take it to the next level. I treated her poorly and like she was expendable, but was "surprised" when she decided to move on. I was blinded by stupidity, youth and ego (… story of my younger days.) Regardless of how badly I treated her or how confused I was about what I deserved, the end result was that I assumed all of this had happened because I was too trusting. As a result, trusting became a hard task for me. In every relationship, I constantly hinted to my partners that replacing them wasn't a big deal. It was my defense. For a period of my life, I always kept in contact with someone from my past so I could run to them every time I needed to prove to my current fling I always had options, I always had a fallback. I never wanted to face the embarrassment of being cheated on again.

History

They say women are like cats and men are like dogs

They believe "When you kick a woman, she goes away and never comes back but a man will come back no matter what"

But I beg to differ

Any soul on fire with love will keep going back to where the fire started

But it wasn't love that kept me running into the arms of the ladies of my past

It was them catching me every time I was falling

History kept us connected

Every time my plan A failed, I had to revert back to plan B

Unfamiliar with the feeling of being single, I had to find a backup after every relationship

Rebounding to the women I knew would let me enter their lives and help my broken heart feel whole again

Back to the women I knew who still let me into their lives, into their hearts, into them

History had me with a phone full of contacts to keep in contact just in case me and my girlfriend lost touch

These women were the women good enough to sleep with but weren't good enough to be in a relationship with

History kept me going back to who I knew wouldn't hurt me

What I knew would help me numb the pain even though I was bringing more destruction upon my heart

I kept coming back because I felt I had authority over them

Their feelings for me were evident

Their willingness to please me was comforting

So when they said no, I ran back into their hands

I didn't keep coming back because the love I had between me and them raised fire in my bones, but because they were the only ones who would give the dog in me a bone

History was the reason

Because never have I intended for these women to be my reason to love

Everyone saw us together
They complimented us
I fell for you
You were the prize that was always on my arm
My friends couldn't believe that I let my guard down
You were the best I've ever had
Wise ones told me to never lose you
The foolish ones even said you were a good choice
But then, you walked away
In public, I felt like a walking shame
I would feel the eyes watching me and the mouths
gossiping about me
People would even question me
"Oh you guys aren't together anymore?"
They act like they feel sorry for me, but I can see their
second face mocking me
It was too good to be true they thought
Too true to believe for me
A good thing escaped my grip
Although what I felt for you is gone
These feelings I will keep holding
The love definitely reached its dead end
But I can't lose, I was born to win

Pride won't let me move on

PorNO

I met you on a hot summer day

One of my friends introduced you to me

Then you were something so foreign to me in comparison to now

I never knew the power you would have over me

Never knew how you would kill my desire for intimacy and chemistry

Replace them with pure hunger for simply sex

You convinced me that my penis was the only heart I needed

You corrupted me

I have yet to find out how you got this far involved in my life

I let you in on that hot summer day

Since you kept devouring my purity to pieces

Contributed to me seeing women as sex objects more than I realized

You taught me to freely give in to temptation

Taught me a quick thing about pleasure through masturbation

You convinced me to listen to my hormones and that women weren't good enough unless they had big butts and big breasts

I kept giving what could've been a gift to my wife over and over to you

I became your slave, a soul who only thirsted for orgasms

You blinded me, caused me to have false expectations in relationships

You dehumanized me, killed my desire for love

You are an enemy who presents yourself as pleasure, as a teacher, as part of what is normal

You planted lust inside my heart

You damaged me spiritually and emotionally but since pleasure was involved I grew to love you instead of saying no to the self-destruction

I hate you

Pornography restructured my mind. Without it, lust would have never ruled me as much as it did. I started watching porn in search of pleasure. I was a young kid with hormones raging. It was the only way to make masturbation fun. Men are visual and without porn, masturbation is sometimes insufficient. As I grew older, I became addicted to watching pornography and masturbating. It became the high I could get at any given time. Everyone was doing it, everyone talked about it – the pleasure we could access anytime. Throughout my college years, I couldn't live without it. Porn became so addictive that I would take breaks and run to a restroom to watch it and masturbate away. Because of it, I also became a sex addict. I reached a point in my life where I didn't necessarily care who I was sleeping with, as long as it was a woman. I craved sex. I wanted to do everything people in the porn videos did, and I wanted to do it as often as I could. I never wanted to get my feelings involved with any woman, really. I only wanted sex. I wanted to experiment and do the things in those videos. I wanted women who would let me do anything, so I could get close to mimicking those men I saw. I spent hours searching for women who would just want sex. Anything good in my life revolved around sex during those days.

Interestingly enough, I never mentioned this addiction to the women I actually dated. All throughout this addiction everything in me felt something was wrong. I would mention it to no one although it was the biggest part of my life. Also, none of the women I dated cared for porn. Many of them actually disliked it. One of my girlfriends once caught me watching porn and told me that she felt as if she wasn't doing a good enough job. She felt bad that I had to go look at other women and do it myself. At the time I almost agreed with her, but didn't because I needed a girlfriend; I needed sex. It wasn't until I started my spiritual journey, that I began seeing it through her eyes; how watching those girls was a form of adultery in my heart, an affair that made her feel insufficient and unworthy.

My relationships throughout that time were mostly great. During those times, fornicating was the norm for me. The first stages of most of my relationships would be fine because we would have plenty of sex. However, I would later become bored. The excitement of being able to sleep with someone I began to care for would die, which is normal because most partners start to feel unhappy when they are in the wrong relationship past the "honeymoon stage." But my problem was bigger. My problem was sex. The women would provide it and the sex would be spectacular, but I always felt as if I couldn't treat them like the women in the videos. I would feel limited in the relationship. I would feel unhappy because I couldn't have a girlfriend who acted like the women in the videos. The thought of having a woman as a sex object excited me more than anything I could do with my actual girlfriend. So I would resort to cheating. I would search online or at parties to pick up other girls I thought would be freaky enough to do anything. Something in me wanted a woman with no attachment who I could mistreat and use only for sex. I grew to find satisfaction in women who had no respect for themselves, women who would easily agree to my movie-derived fantasies.

It wasn't until enough of my relationships were destroyed and I became a single, born-again Christian practicing celibacy, that I began noticing the impact porn had on me. It wasn't because I became spiritual that I noticed the destruction, it was because I finally begin abstained from porn and sex. As I abstained from porn, the desire to love women and treat them as more than objects grew in my heart. Seeing them as objects who existed for the purpose of sex only became nonsense to me. I began to crave love. It wasn't simply a transformation of becoming mature, but a renewal in my heart. For every video I watched, I would download inside of me this idea that women are for that purpose and to treat them that way. I was seeing women through the lenses of porn. Every time I saw a woman I would envision the things I'd seen in porn that I could do to her. Eventually, pleasure became more than just sex.

The effect porn was having on me is happening to others. It's building in people the desire for sex and nothing more. Lust-filled hearts,,. So many more promiscuous young men and young women, so many more people unable to commit. The basis of many relationships now is good sex and interestingly enough, it isn't guaranteed that your partner will stay loyal to you when there's a guy or a gal out there who will fulfill their lustful fantasies.

Abstaining from porn has been fulfilling, but not an easy journey. Without consistently putting up a fight and denying myself and reminding myself what it did to me it's easy to give into to it. It's a battle that can be overcome, but you have to remind yourself that addictions often try to creep their way back into people's lives. You have to stay guarded and protect yourself from being lured into something so destructive. When or if you fail, get back up and keep on fighting.

Say no more to chasing the bad girls, and pursue yourself a good woman.

Say no more to playing baby daddy, and become a father.

Say no more to shacking up with different girls and dating around, and commit to a real woman. Build yourself a family.

Commitment

She asked me "Where is this going"?

My brain suddenly replied "Nowhere."

But my lips chose to not follow my brain's lead

Like a broken GPS, I had no sense of direction.

But I couldn't give her that impression.

I am a man and I ought to lead

But inside of me the fear of uncertainty whispered to me that I wasn't good enough

I was a college dropout who was supposed to be smart enough

To rise above the statistics.

Statistically I dropped below average

Trying to keep up with the image...

Of a man with a plan

But I wasn't a man according to these failed plans

I slowly replied "I don't know, babe, let's just go with the flow"

In my head I knew going with the flow was for dead fishes, those who couldn't swim.

There's no way I will make it known that I was against going with the current

Didn't want to sound as if I was afraid of commitment

And even if I uttered a word contrary to what I said she would hear the insecurity in my voice

If I dared tell her I wasn't ready

She would conclude that I wanted her to take no part of my future

How I can't possibly mean the "I love you's" I said to her because love is forever

Never would I sit her down and tell her that I feel like a failure

I know she would reply back faster than a speeding bullet emptying these words out of her mouth "But I love you anyways, the money doesn't matter because all I care for is you"

But I don't love me where I'm at, feeling parked on the wrong side of life

It's too early for me to grasp the thought of having a wife

The commitment issues in me live not because I am still finding enjoyment in messing around with other women.

It's because the fear of not being man enough reigns in me.

I can't provide for anyone when on my own I'm just getting by

Instead of living I'm just letting time go by

But commitment is still my nightmare

The question continues to echo in my head and it dawns on me that this is truly going "nowhere"

At least for now....

A man afraid of **committing** to a woman for the **wrong** reasons will drop the fear of commitment when he finds the **right** woman worth **committing** to.

Many men are afraid of commitment because they aren't ready to let go of their promiscuous ways and their lifestyle of fun as defined by the majority. Clubs are their favorite place in the world, drunk nights are the moments they cherish, drugs are their escape, sex numbs their pain, and money makes their souls feel alive. They don't want to feel chained, limited and whipped by what they think is love when in reality they're stuck in a relationship with a woman who lacks understanding, who isn't yet mature enough to not settle for less than what she's worth.

Some men are afraid of committing because they see themselves in no shape to build a future with someone else. Some are insecure about where they are in life and how far they are from their goals. They don't want to bring a struggle to the table. They want to be stable and comfortable in life first. They don't want to feel as if they aren't man enough. They want to be able to protect and provide without bringing the woman they love into failure with them.

To the man stuck in that situation: She loves you, she wants you. The most valuable thing you can give a woman whose heart belongs to you is your time and affection. You are getting in your own way, not your financial status or failures. Many couples start where you're at and make it. Some couples even start out poor and become rich together. Teamwork makes dreams work. All you need is love – it's the glue that will make the teamwork become effortless.

To the woman in that situation: You might be clueless and just now realizing that's how he feels. Quit fishing for his reassurance over and over that you will be part of his future. You're worth being committed to, and the problems he has are inner issues that he needs to solve himself. I know you do love him and you believe together you will survive but to him that is just a thought, a thought with no hope. The more you ask him, the more it triggers anger inside of him. He is constantly reminded that he is a failure and how he is delaying great things. You are picking an unhealed wound, so be patient. Do not wait forever but do wait. Just remember that it's not your responsibility to fix a broken man. It's not worth your time, your effort, your love or your tears. If he's not willing to fix himself for you, there's nothing left to do but walk away and move beyond his selfish, immature, and ultimately abusive behavior. Not all men are broken, but you have to believe you deserve better. Expect better and you'll receive better, it's that simple.

Commitment without intent of marriage is a bad contract.

Thank You, Celibacy

Thank you for showing me the beauty of patience
It is truly a virtue
Patiently waiting to connect my soul with one who I was
meant to give myself to
Thank you for appeasing the lustful desires and
strengthening my grip on self-control
Before you, I was a beggar
Begging for attention, validation, short-term pleasure from
women who weren't born to be mine
To the truth, I was blind
Couldn't make love to their minds because their halves
weren't meant to be connected to mine
You freed me from the lies about love
 Thinking love was a game that would keep ending quickly
after all these quickies
You saved me from the stronghold my hormones had over
me that lied to me and told me what is in my pants wasn't
supposed to be controlled
I was made a prostitute
 Lust had me giving myself to random strangers, pimping
myself and paying me with conceit and acceptance
"No," I said to you, thinking it was weak for me to be pure
and do what's right and commendable to God.

You helped me reject the system men followed that validated them and made them believe they were real men

It's not always easy but the journey with you is more than worth it. As I continue to build a friendship with you it gets easier.

I thank you for helping me achieve things I never knew I could do...

Like wait for my wife

Like changing my thought process to believing that sex is designed to be a bonus when you find that special person to spend your life with

Like fight to look away when a good-looking woman flaunting her body passes by

Thank you! Through GOD you've restored me and giving me the strength to keep on fighting to wait for my beautiful bride.

If you would've mentioned celibacy to me back in my college days, I might have laughed at you and probably called you a fool. Sex was my go-to. Sex was my pain killer, it fulfilled my appetite, and it was all I had. In relationships, I was the freak. I was the addict. Celibacy was so foreign to me I couldn't even pronounce the word. On my journey to spiritual restoration, I began this journey of celibacy. It's one of the best choices I've ever made. It's been hard and very challenging but it was the right thing to do. It has helped me gain a clarity and balance I didn't believe possible. So many of the people I thought I was in love with were just used for sex. It's only now that I can see that reality and admit it. No different than any path of self-control I take, it is extremely hard. I've lost against it, but I chose to never stay down. I was reminded that I must fight daily to win against something I once lived for. . If you're on the same page and fall short, do not give up. Get back up. Do not condemn yourself. Continue pressing towards the mark.

We can't tell women to keep their legs closed and tell men to take their pants off as often as they can. That is a double standard and a foolish ideology. It's just as right for a man to practice purity and wait for his wife.

I hate you

I hate the pain you introduced me to

Emotions powered by feelings I never knew

You got tired of what I put you through, so you left and now we're through

I hate you for having me believe that you would stand up for me, but when the time came, you couldn't hold me down

They say a good woman is the backbone of the relationship, but when my back was against the wall, it was like you had scoliosis

You couldn't help but kick me to the curb and backstab me until the knife pierced through my heart

I hate you for listening to your family and friends more than you listened to my heart screaming "I'm hurt, give me a little time please, it's you who I want"

...Nope

I never undermined the wisdom your mother whispered to your sensitive ears

But it killed us the times she yelled "get rid of him" because he's not good enough

I was quietly hated, highly doubted, consistently judged and pretentiously loved

I don't hate you for valuing your family and friends over me

I hate you for de-valuing me because of them

I hate you for not being direct

For having a vocabulary full of silent letters when it came to communicating

A voice full of hints, I felt as if your emotions were sign language, and I was a blind man trying to interpret everything

Our communication was off until we did things that turned each other on

I hate you. I hate you. I hate you.

But in reality, I hate me more

I hate me for demanding from myself what I couldn't deliver

I hate me for not stepping up and doing what was necessary to fix what needed to be fixed

I hate me for being so passive and careless

In the process of hating you for all that went wrong, I began to hate myself even more

Hating who I am and hating my mistakes

Hating my choices and hating all that led to us being where we ended

Hating you was simply the manifestation of the anger, hurt, and disappointment that I had

"I hate you" is simply "I love you" clouded by fear and doubt

We hide our pain to keep us from getting hurt again. In the process we hurt people who never aimed to hurt us.

You tried to figure me out as a man
I tried to understand you as a woman
We fell into the land of assumptions
Rivers of complication
Perplexed by the contradictions
We tried to put the pieces together working on the
wrong puzzle
Focusing on the wrong solutions because we didn't see
the real problem
The problem was we were adding all our bad
experiences into the mix trying to solve things
You treated me the way you treated your ex because
you were scared to get hurt again, but I didn't hurt
you the first time
I treated you as I would've treated my ex because I
didn't want to be fooled again, but you weren't the one
who made a fool out of me before
You thought I was in it for your body and I thought
you were trying to control my mind
So our souls were left out...
We were connecting the wrong dots, working on the
wrong puzzle this whole time

The Wrong Puzzle

I am also Human

The tears you don't see are shed when no one's around

Those tears found their way to my eyes when my pain found its way to the center of my heart

I feel pain too

Sometimes I find it hard to stay sane, emotionally, I find it hard to maintain

My past often visits me to break down the door to my peace and sabotage my happiness

I'm haunted by betrayal

I have trust issues because of the knives that are not yet removed from my back

I've been used, abused and confused

I've been bullied into this robot I've become

I am human

If you look closely you'll see the scars

You'll see the insecurities, the bitterness, cries for love and affection

If I let you see past these eyes and into my soul,

You'll see past the tough guy's defense, the heartless warrior's façade

You'll see how I am afraid that I'll be hurt again

Afraid I'll never be whole again

I had to make up my character

It had to be fictional, but believable

I had to go through the motions, play the role and act it out

All I'm asking for is love and compassion

Craving for a love that will cause me to open up and be free again

Love that will overfill my soul until the demons spill out of my inner being

Trust me-- I don't want to stay this way

Wasn't born with this poker face

Wasn't born this way

Believe in me and love me

That's all I truly long for

I promise you as I mature and heal, this tough guy image will wash off

I am a man

I am human

I fell in love with a white girl,
Tried dating "my own kind," tried falling for a Haitian girl, but my feelings kept tripping
So, I fell in love with a white girl
Gave my heart to a Hispanic girl, but we were too different
She was spicy and I was calm
She was loud and I was sometimes mistaken for a mute
So I fell in love with a white girl
But her family believed that my brown skin was too dark to welcome into the family
The black in me was destined to go down a dark path, or so they believed
But still, I had already fallen for a white girl
That's what everyone else saw, but I saw a woman I was able to relate to, someone who was part of the human race
I saw a soul I was willing to love
Love is color-blind, but so many are blinded by colors
To help those blind to their ignorance, those who seem to have no clue that we all bleed, that we all feel pain, that we are all human and death is the end of us all
I tell them, "I fell in love with a white girl and her folks didn't like my skin tone"

Fell in love with a white girl

Dear good guy

I can hear your cries

I can feel your pain

I can smell your frustration

I can see the confusion in your eyes

Confused about how women see you

In a land of women tired of being played

They still take you as a joke and think you're all games

They play you like they were played

They can't see the seriousness in your eyes

When you call her "Queen" and ask for her heart

And you cry for commitment, they back out and shut down

Treat you like the bad guys treated them

It's so ironic

You hate seeing these ladies get their hearts stomped on

Their minds toyed with

It's killing you because you've done it to women yourself
you've seen other guys do it

You want to save them from the destruction

But like a child who refuses to obey their mother's wisdom, until they are wise enough to understand through experience

They won't value you until they get burned playing with the fire of curiosity

Some of them crave destruction

They crave the fun that these fellas who will degrade them have to offer

They are being guided by curiosity and their wisdom is foolishness

Fight the urge to become like the men these ladies who lack understanding chase after

Don't let rejection consume your heart and cause you to crumble

Being a promiscuous man who lacks self-respect and morals is overrated

Find peace with being the underdog

Your type is needed in this world, my good friend

Hold on

There are women out there who are in search for someone like you

One of them will be the one who appreciates the detailed things about you the previous women called corny

There are women out there who will value your honesty, your character, your loyalty

Hold on, my friend

Narrow is the right path

You are on the right path, my friend

Your time will come in due time

You will not just be getting a girl, you will be getting a woman who will be willing to finish off this life's journey with you

You are not alone

I am with you and I understand the hardships you face, the doubt, the anger

I want you to know you are doing a great job at being you

Do not give up

Stand firm and continue to be different

You will be an example to many although you are in the minority

Corruption seems to be the sweetest fruit to our lips in this day and age. People seem to flirt with the idea of cherishing the good, but then, run to the bad with open arms. Being a man of valor, a "good guy," is something that takes dedication. It takes finding yourself, self-control, will power, prayer and being in tune with your creator. All it takes consistency. Consistently rejecting the ways of the majority, the image society continues to force upon you, rejecting temptations and the feeling of being inadequate and underappreciated.

The pressure to give up is more intense than most believe. I've been a good and bad guy, and I can honestly say, being the bad guy is far more fulfilling when it comes to the senses. However, it doesn't fill the void in you. Hedonism won't fill the love you lack within you, nor will it fill your love tank. It won't give you real joy or peace. People don't see how hard it is to swallow your pride and say no to the fun most males choose to partake in. Many don't see how enticing it is. It's hard to fight and to be okay with looking weak in the eyes of fools, or looking too soft in the eyes of the prideful, or too insufficient in the eyes of the critics.

Being a good guy takes discipline, but it's worth it. Men are quick to mock other men who say no to women who are throwing themselves at them. They make the man with morals feel like a coward; a loser for rejecting a woman. Women partake in the mocking as well. Many make a laughing stock out of the good guys, ridicule their polite approach to women; their gentleness and faithfulness. Good guys are punks in their eyes and aren't challenging enough. Good guys are the minority. They are the dying breed of this generation. We live in a generation that applauds the bad more than it commends the good. I haven't been a good guy all my life, but I can tell you that I'm striving daily to be a better man and that being a better man of GOD is challenging. To my fellow gentlemen striving to do so, hold on. Don't give up.

You told me you would never stop loving me.

As a man, I thought it was final since women tend to be more serious about what they say to men.

However, women also utter words fueled by emotions, and emotions are inconsistent.
But you consistently convinced me that we were meant to be.
You made me believe that this thing between us would always be.
You left me when I thought everything was going right.
We could've been champions together. I could've given you a ring, but you vanished without a fight.
Was your heart invested, or were you just curious?
Were you curious to see how much of me you could convert to being a lover of yours?
I was a teammate who was willing to work with you and win at this thing called love.
I was a believer who believed in you.
I was a broken soul who was willing to work to be whole with you.
How could it be? It was so difficult for you to say, "I love you," because you, "had to be sure."
How was it so easy for you to say, "I'm not sure about us," from the same heart?
You had me doubting what you meant when you said you would never stop loving me.
Love was supposed to be the glue that kept us together and kept us going...
But it all stopped-- a dead end.
I put you first only to come last.
How could you walk away that easily?
How could our love end that quickly?

I keep trying to put it all together,
but I kept falling apart.
Instead of trying to figure it out,
I decided to figure ME out and let life sort it out.
You played me with the words, "I love you."
Unfortunately, I believed you.
You left me feeling like a fool.
I guess it's karma since I imagine I too left a few women
feeling this way
I wish you would've warned me.

This is where I stopped.

Write His Wrongs

I wasn't a man when we met. I was a lost boy trying to find himself.
I'm sorry for convincing you that I was one when I wasn't.
I'm sorry that you invested your time into nothing.
All you got from us being together was an experience.
I said all the good things you needed to hear so that you could be convinced that your heart was being handled by someone who would be devoted to protecting it
Instead of handing you mine in return, I guarded it. I built walls as great as the wall of China around it.
I waited until you invested enough of your trust in me, then I decreased the value of your stock.
I started to abuse your trust, verbally harmed you and left your heart bruised and broken.

I wasn't a man.
I was a hurt soul carrying around all the bad of my past on my shoulders.
I was confused.
I put on a façade that I was a healed guy who'd overcome so much struggle,
But I was holding onto the things that cut me the deepest.
So, when you asked for a piece of my soul, I served you the rotten part.

What I gave you was a dark part of me that would cause anyone to fall apart.
In your cup, I poured the revenge that overfilled my heart from the girls before you.
I did to you what was done to me.
I hurt you.
I gave you deep scars, way beyond superficial...

I wasn't a man.
I was a fool who didn't know what, "I love you" meant.
I thought it was a product of good sex, so, when we had sex was the only time I felt comfortable enough to let it roll off my tongue.
My heart used to skip beats when I saw you.
It wasn't the butterflies, but my hormones raging inside when my eyes saw you.
The lust in my heart craved you
I had you believing that I was in love with you when I simply lusted after you.
I was taking away your precious womanhood; leaving you stranded, as if you were another to add to my body count.

I wasn't a man
I was a kid afraid of commitment
A boy still looking to play boyfriend, unwilling to pursue you
I saw our relationship as a short sprint, instead of being in it for the long run
I wasted your time talking about marriage to feed you false hope that would keep you hungry for more of me

I uplifted you when I needed a lift, kept you encouraged
when I knew we were going nowhere
I fed you lies to make you feel on top of the world, and
then put you down with my actions

I am sorry. This is my apology to you... to every ex who was
ever part of my life.... to every woman who gave
themselves to me with great hope that I would be
different. To the women I've hurt, used, manipulated and
left without hesitation, I'm sorry to you. To the women I
influenced to settle because I helped them believe they
were good enough to sleep with me, but not good enough
to be in a relationship with me. To the women I sold the
good guy image when in reality, I was a wolf in sheep's
clothing, I am sorry. I am sorry for contributing to you
losing yourself in search of finding myself. I'm sorry for
breaking your hearts just because mine was broken. I am
sorry for the man who I was to you. I pray each one of you
find the king you deserve. I pray you never settle for a man
like the one I was to you. I pray you find peace with your
past and live the future with a healed heart. I pray you
become open to love and you find a man who is more than
willing to love you and be open to you. Once again, I
wasn't a man, but a boy doing what he thought men
should do. I am sorry.

I Wasn't Ready

I destroyed our relationship because I wasn't ready

Ready to be happy with one woman

Ready to commit myself to someone and walk the journey of growing as one

I wasn't ready for all the good memories we would have

The new chapters we would write together

I wasn't ready to be loved and accepted by you
I wasn't ready to sacrifice all of me to gain all of you
I wasn't ready for a beautiful love story

It was all too good to be true, and I was used to what's bad enough to believe

It was fear and immaturity working deep down inside of me

Doesn't make sense for me to turn down such a good thing

But it's hard when everything I've had similar to that ended up in destruction

Curiosity was still in my bones looking for some new experiences

The fun only a single man can have

"No matter how good of a woman you are, you will never be enough for a man who is not ready"

– Unknown

In many cases, I wasn't prepared for a solid relationship, nor was I willing to invest the effort into building one. This led to me counting down the days until the end, rather than working towards better days in the relationship. Many times, we make emotional decisions without thinking. We don't evaluate before we finalize things. We want something, and we act on the desire for that moment. We convince ourselves that we are ready for something until we are hit with the reality of what it means to have it.

Many of my relationships were purposely destroyed in this way. I was excited by the idea of dating, and in love with the idea of love, yet, not ready for it. Accordingly, I found no motivation to be consistent in a relationship. I purposely did things to end some of my relationships when I realized what I'd gotten myself into. It's unfortunate that some of those partners were ready, and ended up being hurt. Never did I lie, however, I simply went in with good intentions, yet, my true desires were still desires that pertained to the single life. Both men and women make mistakes like mine going into relationships, and that is the reason why the fire in the start sometimes dies out. Sometimes, the problem is simply people not being ready. There's no motivation to make themselves ready enough to work things out.

The Woman of My Life

You are what I've been waiting for

I've traveled a long journey waiting on my official love story to start

Waiting on the day for us to connect from an unusual spark

Wow, you're beautiful

With a heart empty of love, the few times I mentioned love, it felt empty

I can't wait to use this word to describe you

You aren't perfect, but you are a perfect fit for me

You are intelligent, confident, strong, loyal, funny, caring, gentle, wise...and so many more great things I can think of when I think of you...

I've laid down my life of foolish living and being led by curiosity involving other women for you.

I've made plenty of mistakes, and failed countless times, but I know with you, I will apply the lessons I've learned.

These walls will come down for you

This heart will belong to you

I will lust for you, and you only

Faithfulness will not be a gift from me to you, but how things ought to be

I will honor you 'til the end of my days as we honor God.

I am grateful that you are my backbone, my rib, the coverage over my heart

I am thankful that you chose to love me despite me being me

I've had great moments and life-changing experiences that led me to being this hopeless romantic

I can only imagine what our love story will be like

I promise not a fairy tale; I am not saying this thirst to love you will make things easy

I promise you that I will fight hard, that I will protect our relationship...

I will flee from temptations, think before I decide, and always keep you first behind our Lord.

I will never let my past define our future, neither will I let your past harm our present

I cannot wait to meet you

I love you

You are the woman of my heart, my future wife.

Fall in love with your future spouse before that future becomes present. The power of positive affirmations is something I've learned enhances positive events in our lives. You can indeed speak things into existence as long it's peppered with wisdom and not foolishly and selfishly desiring things that go against GOD's will for you. All the experiences I've faced in relationships only brought me closer to desiring a wife. All the times I was hurt, or hurt someone, cheated, was cheated on, and all the arguments, breakups, the good and bad...all led me to wanting to do it right with someone else. I want to do something else with the right one.

A lot of us men want love, but because we lack love, we act unloving sometimes. We want love, but we are also tired of getting it wrong and it seems too many of us can't stop getting it wrong even when it's our choice. We become victims of our mistakes to a point where we become pessimistic about love--the very thing we desire. After we've experienced enough and matured to a certain level, all we desire is something real to hold on to forever. We do not voice it, because it sounds like a fairy tale coming from our lips. It sounds like weakness rolling off our tongues, but in those times, when loneliness is at our doorsteps and we are deep in our thinking, all we really want is that one girl who we are sure will love and respect us. Many of us can't wait until the time comes that we love someone enough to lie down our lives for them.

Dear Son

Do not allow society to define you.

The man society will try to mold you into is socially created, controlled, inauthentic, insensitive, womanizing, and unproductive towards the betterment of our world.

1.) Do not allow yourself to be lured into the ways of fools and be enticed by all the materialistic things males use to shape their identities.

2.) Believe not that success is buried in women and fame.

3.) Respect yourself enough to respect others, for what is within you, is what will project out of you.

4.) It is honorable to be faithful to one woman at a time.

5.) Falling in love is greater than any orgasm without attachment. As a matter of fact, love will enhance orgasms.

6.) It is foolish to act as if you are immortal and without feelings. Being sensitive is okay, being nice is commendable, and being respectful is a great trait. Have dignity and be grateful.

7.) Women are God's gift to men. You are not God's gift to them. Cherish your good woman when you find her. If you treat her like a queen, she will have no trouble devoting her life to her king.

8.) Justify not your lies rather do what is necessary to grow in those areas

9.) Pride will assassinate every good thing that enters your life. Do not let your ego rule over you.

10.) Experiences are teachers. Do not allow the lessons to pass you by.

11.) God is not the enemy. A God fearing man is a man of valor no matter what society may say.

I have learned that the opposite of all these things will make life more painful. You will have to go on your own journey to conclude that these things are true, but I promise to be by your side until death separates me from you. I cannot wait to build a relationship with you. I love you, and I haven't even met you yet. You are my prize. I promise to be a leader in your life, and a positive example from whom you can learn...but via my words, and by exemplifying a moral lifestyle. You're the son of the King of Kings, so be a victor. Rise above the norm, be the change you want to see in the world rather than wasting your energy complaining about it. Be great, for greatness lies within you.

A man is not supposed to be an animal. Strength doesn't lie in how little pain he shows, but in how he handles the pain he feels. Be a man. Be real with yourself. Be human.

Dear Daughter

First and foremost, I love you. I will love nothing on the face of this earth more besides GOD and your beautiful mother. Because I love you, I will protect you in ways you will hate. I will make decisions for you that you will think are ludicrous. You will hate me at times, but in those times, please understand that they are an act of love.

I promise to raise you and not let television, school and society raise you.

I promise you to be your first love. I will be the first man to make you feel valued and worthy. I will be the first man to remind you that you are smart, push you to be goal-driven; the first man to reassure you that you are loved.

I promise you to show you love exists and show you beauty and the ugly parts of marriage.

I promise to teach you the ways of the Lord, not by setting rules for you to obey, but by setting an example through lifestyle. I promise to be a godly man in my actions and not just my words.

Know this...

You are beautiful, but you're also intelligent

You were created by a brilliant master who had a plan for you, even before you were conceived

You are worth more than anything anyone can afford

You are important

You are full of purpose

You will not find yourself in compliments of man, relationships, sex, drugs or anything outside of you

You are loved, my love

You deserve the world, My Dear. Don't settle for a man who can only treat you to a motel room

Never compromise for acceptance

You are worthy of greatness.

A Real Father

Instead of letting the world abuse you, let God use you!

You were someone I knew of, but never *knew*

Always fascinated by the idea of your existence but with so many roads I never knew which one to take to find you

I lived life according to my own manual, even though you left me your copy

I tried to live life solely by my intellect, and ended up outsmarting myself

I wondered where you were during so many events in my life that you could have saved me from

I wondered why it took so much to please you

Until I met you at this random church, at this little town

I knew this beautiful meeting was meant to be.

I've been to plenty of places where they said they know you and the different types of you, but this one was different, you were *you*

You spoke up, and I had an experience that I've never had

But I was too young for that in my thinking

Too much living to do to choose the path of righteousness

My flesh longed for the things that were against you, and I didn't feel as if obeying you was the way to go

I went on and lived my own life, according to my own will, for my own benefit

I followed my own instructions to get to where I wanted and ended up being disappointed

We came to meet at my darkest hours

When I became all sexed-out, smoked out, drunken out, drained out and completely defeated in and out

I decided to give our relationship a try

You were the only person I knew who would never stop loving me even when everyone else, including myself, stopped loving me

You took me back with open arms

You washed me clean

You told me if I followed you, you would land me where I needed to be

The old sinner in me was put to death and I became your child, saved by grace.

You installed your wisdom within me as I made a fellowship with you

Without you, I wouldn't be this man without you, I wouldn't be living this plan

Without you, my eyes wouldn't be so open, and I wouldn't have any light in me to share with this world

Oh Father, how I love you

You take me as I am

imperfect and willing to help me grow out of my imperfections as long I do not use "I'm perfect as an excuse" and follow your son, my beautiful savior

You lead me to do better as long as I don't use, "Only God can judge me" as a cop out

You are the reason I'm here and the reason I'm going where I'm going

From the bottom of my heart, all I can say is, I love you, Father.

I thank you for sending your son to help me become your son

Without you this version of me, would be as fictional as most people believe you to be

I will continue with you, continue to grow, and continue to love you

Thank you

Dear you

You are a better man than you think you are.

You've fought so many battles and endured so many losses, but also tasted a fair amount of victory.

Listen to me, DO NOT GIVE UP!

You are great. You are strong and you are a good man.

So what? You lived like a fool before. You made foolish decisions. You fooled people and fooled yourself. Those foolish days led to you being wiser.

Don't look at the past or get too caught up trying to be the man you imagine to be.

Don't give an ear to the people who knew the old you, who are looking at the new you and yelling hypocrisy.

Remember they don't live with you. They don't know your heart, and they aren't looking for change in you.

Them being stuck with the, "you" of the past is their problem, not yours.

The opinions of those who cannot applaud who you're becoming and striving to become are irrelevant.

I am proud of you.

Keep striving for greatness, my friend.

To be continued...

CONTACT

Pierre Alex Jeanty

Email

contact@gentlemenhood.com

gentlemenhood@gmail.com

Website

www.gentlemenhood.com

Social Media

Twitter.com/gentlemenhood

Instagram.com/gentlemenhood

Facebook.com/gentlemenhood

Booking

321-961-5302

51398717R00080

Made in the USA
San Bernardino, CA
21 July 2017